Original title:
Minty Memoirs

Copyright © 2025 Creative Arts Management OÜ
All rights reserved.

Author: Riley Hawthorne
ISBN HARDBACK: 978-1-80566-682-0
ISBN PAPERBACK: 978-1-80566-967-8

Fragrant Journeys

In a garden of grass, I stopped to sniff,
A dandelion sprouted, gave quite a whiff.
A bee buzzed by, with a hilarious dance,
I burst out laughing, it took quite a chance.

With mint on my breath, I rode a blue bike,
Chased by a squirrel—it was quite the hike.
We raced through the park, but the squirrel won,
As I sat on a bench, sighed, 'Well, that's fun!'

The Essence of Time

I found an old jar, filled with scents of yore,
Pine and lavender, oh what a score!
A whiff of old cheese made me chortle and giggle,
'Were these the aromas that made grandpa wiggle?'

As I brewed up tea with a sprig of delight,
The kettle whistled loud, it took off in flight!
Did the room smell of laughter, or was it just me?
With a grin like a cat, I felt so free.

Flourish of Forgotten Times

Old perfume bottles, dusty but bold,
Each scent tells a tale, a mystery told.
A spritz of cologne, and I pictured the dance,
While grandma swayed, giving life a chance.

In a cloud of nostalgia, I nearly did trip,
Over mismatched socks consuming my grip.
Yet in laughter, I found those moments divine,
These fragrant mishaps, oh how they shine!

Aromatic Reminders

A whiff of fresh basil, sprightly and bright,
Brought back my childhood, oh what a sight!
With pizza in hand, I danced with delight,
But tripped on my shoes, oh what a fright!

Each scent that I stumble upon takes me back,
To sock puppet shows and a wild snack attack.
So here's to the flavors that tickle and tease,
Let's all raise a toast to our goofy cheese!

The Spirit of Greenery

In the garden where we'd play,
Chasing shadows day by day.
Leaves as crowns upon our heads,
We danced on paths where laughter spreads.

Bouncing balls and giggles loud,
Whispers soft beneath the cloud.
Nature's secrets hid in grass,
We'd find them all, oh what a class!

Squeaky swings and slides so tall,
With sticky fingers, we would sprawl.
Nature's joy was wild and free,
As we climbed the old oak tree.

Now we laugh at those sweet scenes,
With hopes and dreams like grassy greens.
Each memory, a bright confetti,
Reminds me life was kind of petty.

Vapor Trails of Youth

Remember when the skies were blue,
And every day held something new?
With bicycles and dreams so grand,
We soared like jets around the land.

Our laughter echoed, wild and fast,
As we raced forward, skipping past.
With bubble gum and sneaky pranks,
We'd rule the world with our childlike ranks.

Fizzy drinks and summer nights,
In candy worlds, we'd have our fights.
The smell of popcorn filled the air,
As we'd get lost without a care.

But now, these trails of vapors fade,
Like dreams we dared to serenade.
Yet in my heart, they'll always stay,
Those goofy times of youthful play.

The Cool Embrace of Time

Time's a trickster, oh so sly,
With moments zooming swiftly by.
We'd freeze those frames of joy and cheer,
In ice cream shops, all smiles and beer.

Wrinkled jeans and thrift shop hats,
Dancing cats and talking bats.
Moments wrapped in silly quirks,
Life unfolds with playful jerks.

We'd sit by ponds and share our dreams,
Dreaming big, or so it seems.
Time would wink and fade away,
Yet leaves behind what words can't say.

Now we chuckle at those days,
With grayer hair in funny ways.
Catch me if you can, dear friend,
In laughter's arms, we'll never end.

Reflecting on the Herb

In herby past, we'd sit and plot,
Giggling over what we thought.
The smell of mint, so fresh and sweet,
A fragrance rising from our feet.

We'd brew up dreams in cups of tea,
Finding joy in simple glee.
Each sip would spark a silly toast,
To all the friends we loved the most.

In leafy whispers, we found power,
With laughter blooming every hour.
The garden grew with tales untold,
As our young hearts dared to be bold.

So here's to herbs and happy days,
Where fun and laughter hold their plays.
We twirl through life with zest and flair,
Reliving moments we still share.

Delicate Breaths of Yesterday

In a garden where squirrels play,
I tripped over my shoelace today.
A flower sneezed, oh what a scene!
I laughed so hard, you know what I mean?

The sun was shining, oh what a mood,
But my soda fizzed, it was quite rude!
It sprayed my face like a bubbly mist,
I danced around like I couldn't resist.

With each sip, the world feels bright,
I found an old hat, what a sight!
A butterfly landed on my nose,
And laughed as I twirled, struck my pose.

Chasing shadows of simpler times,
With quirky tales and silly rhymes.
Every hiccup, every cheer,
In this tale of joy, let's be sincere!

The Taste of Time

With every tick, the world spins fast,
I tasted jam, but it slipped at last.
Caught my chin with a big old grin,
Sipped lemonade, felt like a win.

A sandwich flew right off my plate,
Chased it down, it turned out great!
Laughter echoed down the lane,
As birds joined in, quirkier than rain.

A cookie crumb stuck in my hair,
Oh dear, what a flavorful affair!
Time's a treat, sometimes it's odd,
But every bite feels like a nod.

Top hats and pastas twirl with glee,
When I try to juggle, oh can't you see?
Each moment's a snack, each laugh a rhyme,
In the grand feast of silly time!

Sipping on Memories

Sipping soda beneath the sun,
Each burp a tale of laughter spun.
I spilled my drink, it looked like art,
Curious onlookers, I played the part.

Forgotten cookies in the drawer,
Each crumble tells tales of yore.
When life hands you lemons, make a scene,
Dance with joy, act like a queen.

Grandma's stories, minty and sweet,
Make me chuckle as I find my seat.
With every sip, I taste a cheer,
Mixed with the mishaps that brought me here.

Lemon pies and daydreams collide,
With giggle fits I can't seem to hide.
This potion of past fills the air,
As nostalgia sparkles, I'm light as air!

Breezy Lullabies

In a hammock swaying in the breeze,
I dreamt of sandwiches with extra cheese.
The birds sang songs that tickled my ears,
I laughed so hard I nearly shed tears.

A breeze came by, wearing a hat,
I shared a joke with a fluffy cat.
Together we sipped on milky shakes,
As clouds danced by on sweet, silly breaks.

The sun dipped low, giggling in red,
While fireflies tucked me into bed.
With whispered dreams and chuckles wide,
I drifted off, laughter as my guide.

Tomorrow awaits with more to explore,
With tasty tales and joys in store.
Every moment, a lullaby sweet,
In this breezy world, life's quite a treat!

Whiffs of Soft Remembrance

In the garden, I took a whiff,
Of something sweet, it made me stiff.
A minty breeze blew 'round my head,
I laughed so hard, I almost fled.

Each leaf a tale, a time gone by,
With every breath, I felt so spry.
Grandpa's stories in every sprout,
I just can't figure them all out!

My nose delights in green delight,
A scent so sharp, it's pure delight.
I jest and joke with roots so sly,
Who knew my nose could make me cry?

With every step, the laughter grows,
The garden whispers all it knows.
So here's to memories fresh and bright,
With every breath, I take to flight.

Trails of Sweet Green

A stroll along the leafy lane,
I sniff and giggle, what a gain!
The bushes dance, the flowers tease,
Telling secrets with the breeze.

I tripped on thyme, fell in a patch,
A sprout took hold, what a good catch!
With every bump, I laugh and grin,
Who knew green roads could feel like sin?

Each fragrant breeze a playful poke,
It's a magic act, or is it a joke?
Life smells sweeter when you just laugh,
And dance around this quirky path.

With petals swirling, joy's afloat,
In this green paradise, I gloat.
Oh, what fun to roam and play,
In tangy trails where I'll stay!

Essence of Sunlit Paths

The sun beams down on dappled greens,
As laughter echoes in between,
I chase the scent of gleeful days,
With every step, the sunlit plays.

A whiff of joy, a splash of fun,
I skip and swirl, oh what a run!
The air is thick with giggles sweet,
While minty leaves dance at my feet.

Old memories twirl beneath my nose,
Like secret whispers from the rows.
I chase a dream through vibrant hues,
With every sniff, I change my views.

In this blissful, fragrant space,
I find my rhythm, set my pace.
The sunlit paths are paved with cheer,
Where fun and scents are always near.

Fragrant Footsteps

I wander through a minty haze,
With every footstep, laughter plays.
The garden speaks in scents so bold,
A tale of joy, merrily told.

A fragrance hugs me like a friend,
With every whiff, my worries end.
The leaves wiggle, urging me to dance,
In this fresh world, I take my chance.

Each bloom a giggle, bright and loud,
I twirl around, I feel so proud.
The air is thick with funny sights,
As I skip past in pure delights.

With every step, a new prank plays,
In fragrant fields where laughter stays.
So here's to life, fragrant and free,
In silly blooms, I find my glee!

The Sweet Chill of Longing

In the cupboard, secrets dwell,
Frosty dreams, I know them well.
Gumdrop smiles and candy chats,
Wishing for those vibrant hats.

Tickling tongues, a silly race,
Sugar giggles at my face.
Every taste, a cheerful flair,
Craving whispers, sweetened air.

The old jar holds a funny fate,
Twirling memories on a plate.
Hovering over past delights,
Joking with the playful sights.

Chill of flavor, here I stand,
Yearning for that fuzzy band.
With every bite, time bends and sways,
In laughter's grip, I'll always stay.

Sipping Life's Coolness

Chillin' out with fizzy cheer,
Bubbles dance, they draw us near.
Lemon zest with minty tease,
Sips of joy that aim to please.

Jokes bubble up, bright and happy,
Life's a drink, not at all sappy.
Swirling flavors, oh what fun,
Life's a party, no need to run.

In each glass, a twist of fate,
Stirring laughter, it's never late.
Splash of zing with every sip,
A frosty laugh, let's take a trip!

Refreshing moments, drink it in,
Crispy giggles, let's begin.
Sipping life with all our might,
Every bubble feels so right.

Echoes Wrapped in Green

Whispers float on breezy nights,
Grassy giggles, small delights.
Lush and leafy, tales unwind,
Sassy rhymes for hearts entwined.

Lost in scents of nature's zest,
Ticklish thoughts, we're surely blessed.
Dancing leaves, a jolly clang,
In the air, our laughter hangs.

Elixirs of the past we chase,
Funny faces, silly grace.
In every corner, joy does creep,
Echoing dreams that never sleep.

Beneath the trees, we find our glee,
Nature's hugs, so wild and free.
With each gust, our spirits rise,
Wrapped in green, beneath the skies.

The Freshness of Old Times

Nostalgic sips from ancient jars,
Recalling joy beneath the stars.
Sweetened tales from yesteryear,
Juggling smiles and frosty beer.

Underneath the candy glow,
Old jokes linger, soft and slow.
Juicy laughs in every sip,
Tasting memories on the tip.

When days were bright and laughter loud,
Echoes of fun form a crowd.
Frothy drinks with silly slosh,
In our hearts, we always quosh.

So raise your glass to days gone by,
In each bubble, a joyful sigh.
Memories like candy rain,
Sweet refreshment from all the pain.

The Flavor of Days Gone By

In the garden, a taste of cheer,
Sweet surprises are often near.
Lemonade laughs and sunlight beams,
We danced in dreams of sugary schemes.

Butterflies flit with sticky feet,
As candy clouds float down the street.
We'd trade our secrets with a wink,
Then giggle, blush, and sip our drink.

Memories wrapped in chewy bliss,
A juicy moment you can't miss.
Old dimes spent at the candy shop,
We'd savor joy and never stop.

A sprinkle here, a sprinkle there,
Our giggles rise up in the air.
With every bite, we laugh and sigh,
Tasting times that flutter by.

Confections from Nature

In the meadow, sweetness unfolds,
Nature's candy, bright and bold.
Berries bloom where fairies play,
A juicy feast on warm, sunny days.

Crisp apples crunch underfoot,
Like laughter escaping, it's so cute.
Cherry blossoms whisper tales,
Of giggly winds and candy trails.

Oh, licorice vines and honey streams,
Carry us back to childhood dreams.
We frolic where the sugar grows,
Tickled by petals that nature sows.

With every sip of sunshine's warm,
We want to capture the moment's charm.
Laughter's the flavor that we crave,
In nature's sweet embrace, we wave.

The Green Veil of Memory

Under leaves, where whispers grow,
Is where the wisest secrets flow.
Minty tales in the twilight glow,
With every giggle, there's another show.

Time stands still with every bite,
Minty shadows dance in the light.
We hoard the laughter like a prize,
As bubbles rise before our eyes.

Chasing dreams on a green breeze,
Funny moments hidden in trees.
With each twist, a tale takes flight,
Laughter wraps us oh so tight.

Whispers of scent, a playful tease,
A playful world that aims to please.
With every memory, joy will thrum,
In the garden where we come undone.

Petals of Reflection

In a meadow of giggles and cheer,
Petals swirl, bringing memories near.
Each pop of color, a candy kiss,
In delight, we find our bliss.

The daisies dance with a gentle sway,
As laughter echoes through the day.
Every bloom tells a funny fable,
Of silly antics at our table.

Kites soaring high, we chase the sun,
In a world where laughter has just begun.
With jokes on breezes, we fill our hearts,
Like chocolate fountains, we don't want to part.

So let's sip nectar from the skies,
And catch these giggles before they fly.
With petals of joy, we'll make our mark,
Creating memories in the spark.

Cascades of Refreshing Thoughts

In the garden of dreams, I twirl,
Where flavors dance, and giggles unfurl.
A breeze blows whispers, sweet and bright,
Making my worries take flight.

Tasting the moments, sour and sweet,
Replaying the day, it's quite a treat.
With every laugh, I take a sip,
And ride the wave on a memory trip.

In life's crowded space, I trip and fall,
Stumbling over pets, I'm having a ball.
Like peppermint swirls, my thoughts glide,
Through laughter and nectar, I happily ride.

A sprinkle of joy on a mundane day,
In mishaps and giggles, I choose to play.
With every hiccup, a chuckle is born,
In the garden of fun, I am reborn.

Chilling Through the Years

Tickling time with a frosty grin,
The echoes of laughter dance in the din.
As memories flip like a crisp page,
I ride the rollercoaster, uncaged.

Old summer nights with slushies abound,
Who knew that cold could feel so profound?
Frosty adventures in the blazing sun,
With friends by my side, the laughter's begun.

Like ice cream spills that stain the floor,
Each drop tells a tale, who could want more?
Wobbly bikes through the alley we sped,
Chasing the good times, no one took dread.

Years come and go like chill in the air,
But joy's a constant, it's always there.
So here's to the memories, wild and free,
In every frozen giggle, there's a piece of me.

Petals of Past Lives

Plucking petals from whimsical dreams,
Each one a tale, bursting at seams.
With mischief and laughter, I take my share,
Secrets and smiles float in the air.

Dancing through moments that shimmer and spark,
Giggles of days spent late until dark.
Rosy reflections from years gone by,
Riding on nostalgia, we laugh and we sigh.

Petals of joy, petals of woe,
Each one whispers what we used to know.
With blunders and oopses that never cease,
Life's an adventure, a messy release.

In gardens of memory, we roam carefree,
Chasing the echoes, just you and me.
The past is a riot, let's celebrate loud,
With flowers of youth, let's grow ever proud.

Hope Springing from the Soil

From the dirt, a giggle breaks through,
With sprigs of laughter, a brightening hue.
Like seedlings sprouting in April's light,
Every setback turns into delight.

With mud on my hands and joy in my heart,
I plant the seeds of a whimsical start.
A quirky crew of bugs join the show,
As roots entwine where the goofy winds blow.

Patience, they say, is a gardener's muse,
But I find the joy in the silly ruse.
The weeds of doubt just add to the fun,
As hope tumbles forth, a quirky run.

In this wild patch, I dance and I sway,
For the future is bright, come what may.
With chuckles and sprinkles of sunny esteem,
I nurture my dreams, a gardener's dream.

Shadows of Sweet Serenity

In a garden where laughter grows,
Mint leaves whisper secrets, who knows?
The gnomes juggle while singing a tune,
Dancing under the jolly full moon.

Lemonade stands sell imaginary dreams,
With flavors so wild, bursting at the seams.
Silly shadows twist, making us laugh,
As we chase them around the tall grass.

Green Touchstone

A sprig of joy on my sleepy desk,
It winks and it sparks, quite a picturesque mess.
Jars filled with giggles, oh what a sight,
Sipping sunshine, feeling just right.

The cat wears a crown of leafy delight,
As he prowls and pretends he's a knight.
Frogs in top hats hop, oh what a fuss,
All of existence stirs up a plus!

Hints of Bright Forever

Bubbles bounce high in a fizzy parade,
Flavor explosions that never quite fade.
The past is now present, glittering gold,
With tales of adventure forever retold.

Chasing the sun on ice cream blue roads,
Laughter erupts, bursting all codes.
A sprinkle of magic in every bouquet,
Leaving traces of joy in the day.

Cool Narratives

Funky stories swirl in a fresh mint breeze,
While unicorns nap beside the tall trees.
Hiccups of laughter, a candy bazaar,
Where the oddest of dreams are never too far.

Goblins play chess with a deck of cards,
Trading silly riddles while dodging the yards.
An elixir of stories, oh how they mingle,
Creating a world where giggles just tingle.

Scented Memories

When I was young, I found a treat,
A gum so fresh, it swept me off my feet.
I chewed it loud, with glee and delight,
Bubbles popped, a candy-filled flight.

Grandma said, keep that chin up high,
But I just laughed, as clouds floated by.
Her secrets were sweet, in a box by the door,
Lemon and lime, I always wanted more.

That sticky warmth wrapped round my heart,
In every chew, a brand new start.
Each flavor danced, like friends at a show,
In my mind, those memories always glow.

So here's to laughter, and sugary bliss,
In every whiff, I find a kiss.
Those scented days, never too far,
A zingy past, my shining star.

The Breath of Nostalgia

With every puff from that old mint pack,
I'm thrown right back, with a playful whack.
To giggles shared behind the school wall,
Where whispered secrets danced, oh how they'd sprawl.

Each breathy burst, a time machine ride,
A swirl of memories, I can't quite hide.
Sticky fingers and laughter on a spree,
Frolicking youth, just getting free.

That time we dared to steal a few,
Panic and laughter, oh what a crew!
A stolen glance, a cheeky grin,
Back to the days, let the fun begin.

So here's my toast to chaotic fun,
In a world of flavor, we're always young.
With every minty breeze that comes my way,
I giggle anew, as I seize the day!

A Garden of Past Delights

In the garden where flavors bloom,
Lemonade laughter fills every room.
I once found a plant, all green and bright,
It tasted strange, but oh, what a bite!

Frogs in the pond, croaking their tune,
As I chased butterflies under the moon.
Each nibble explored brought giggles galore,
Never knew flavor could open a door.

There's a patch of memories, sweet and wild,
Like candy-floss clouds, I was just a child.
We'd hug up tight and swing with glee,
Sprinkled with laughter, just you and me.

So here's a laugh for the days gone by,
In every crunch, there's a wink to the sky.
A garden of past, with laughter entwined,
Each whiff of those days leaves a grin behind.

Crisp Reflections

In the mirror, I see a cheeky grin,
A youth spent racing with laughter and spin.
With every bite of that cool, fresh treat,
Those moments shine, oh, isn't life sweet?

Boys in the park, with mischief in mind,
Daring each other, the funniest kind.
The minty air, it sparkled and swirled,\nIn our silly games, we conquered the world.

A breath of the past, with giggles galore,
Those crisp recollections, I always adore.
With every chuckle, I'm taken back there,
To the taste of our glee, so light as the air.

So cheers to the laughter, the fun and the cheer,
In the crispness of life, I cherish each year.
With every fresh mint, a playful delight,
Those silly reflections keep my heart light!

Cool Moments Intertwined

In the summer's warm embrace,
We danced in the sunlight's face.
Laughter echoed through the air,
Joyful moments beyond compare.

Ice cream dripped upon my shoe,
You giggled, and I laughed at you.
We raced the breeze, cheeky and free,
Oh, the mischief, just you and me.

Aroma of the Past

Last week's pizza, still on my plate,
With each whiff, I contemplate fate.
Chasing memories, so delightfully odd,
Like that time we thought we were gods.

The scent of cookies, freshly baked,
Hypnotized by all that we caked.
Goofy faces and flour fights,
What a mess, but such sweet sights.

Refreshing Whispers

In a world that swirls with zest,
We find moments that are the best.
A splash of soda, a fizzy cheer,
Everything sparkling when you are near.

Whispers shared under the stars,
We giggled, thinking we were superstars.
Each silly joke, a little prize,
Rolling laughter under the skies.

Sprigs of Time

A stroll down memory lane today,
Found some sprigs where we used to play.
With silly hats and mismatched shoes,
We twirled and spun, made our own news.

Snapshots caught in the summer sun,
Every moment, just pure fun.
Jokes outta nowhere, laughter galore,
With you in my life, who could ask for more?

Memories Infused with Coolness

In a garden of tales, I wandered free,
Lemonade laughter, what a sight to see!
Sneaky squirrels in their furry delight,
Swapping my snacks for a fresh summer bite.

Tickling the daisies, twirling around,
Slipping on sunshine, never a frown.
Ice cream drips down, oh what a mess,
But who needs a napkin in summer's caress?

The bubbles of soda danced in midair,
Whispering secrets with cool summer flair.
Grass stains on jeans that tell me to play,
Reminding my heart it's a fun-loving day.

With fireflies glowing and stars above,
Each moment a treasure, a tale I've loved.
Sugar high giggles escape like a breeze,
Moments like these, oh, they're sure to please!

When Time Tasted Like Herb

Once in a kitchen, spices would sing,
Basil and thyme, what a wondrous fling!
Stirring up chaos with a dash of zest,
Saucy shenanigans, oh what a fest!

Mayo mischief on sandwiches sly,
Pickles like dancers, oh how they fly!
Jars of confessions labeled so bright,
Who knew that a salad could cause such delight?

The clock ticked slowly, time brewed a stew,
With laughter as seasoning, friendships grew.
Delicious memories boiled like a dream,
In a pot of joy, we all were supreme.

Rolls on the table, fresh from the dough,
Eating them quickly, racing the show.
In each silly moment, a laugh to reserve,
A banquet of joy, oh how we deserve!

The Taste of Fresh-Worn Dreams

In soft sunlight's cradle, dreams start to bloom,
Whisking through laughter, banishing gloom.
Chasing a kite with a grin ear to ear,
Finding lost wishes, oh what a cheer!

Crispy fall leaves crunch under my shoe,
Each step a giggle, fresh and anew.
Sundae-sparkled skies, swirling with glee,
Scoops of adventure, just you wait and see!

Pancake stacks wobble like towers of fun,
Jelly beans scatter, oh what a run!
Maple syrup rivers flowing just right,
Swaying in dreams as day turns to night.

Riding the whims of the winds that may blow,
The taste of pure magic, with sprinkles to show.
Wrapping it all in a bow made of cheer,
Each sip of adventure connects us right here!

Whimsy of the Windy Past

Once upon laughter, the wind knows my name,
Whirling through memories, never the same.
Balloons in the sky, floating away,
Chasing our shadows in a bright marigold day.

Kites made of giggles, soaring so high,
Tickling the clouds, oh me, oh my!
Frolicking amid fields, barefoot and bold,
Collecting sweet moments like treasures of old.

Nostalgia's a song on the breeze taking flight,
Whisking us back to the joys of the night.
A carousel spinning with laughter and grace,
In the dance of our youth, we find our place.

So let's raise a toast to the whims of the past,
With cookies and laughter, they always will last.
Bubbles of joy floating high in the air,
In the tale of our lives, they're always there!

Breezes of Bold Beginnings

In a garden where laughter ignites,
Every leaf tells tales of the nights.
Frogs wear tuxedos, ready to dance,
While daisies giggle, caught in a trance.

The breeze whispers secrets, oh so sweet,
Tickling my nose with its playful beat.
A snail in a shell dreams of the sky,
While the sun gives a wink, oh my, oh my!

Juggling bees buzz with humorous grace,
Chasing each other in a wild race.
Ants strut like they own the whole place,
Marching in rhythm, no hint of disgrace.

Thus, in this garden of whimsical cheer,
Every corner brings giggles, my dear.
With nature's own punchlines, don't you agree?
A comic adventure, wild and carefree!

A Breath of Green Reflections

In the shade of the fig tree, we lay,
Where memories bloom and children play.
Grasshoppers hopping, oh what a sight,
In a dance-off beneath the sunlight!

Each breeze carries stories of yore,
Of mischief and giggles, and oh so much more.
The fireflies flicker like tiny lamps,
Drawing out laughter from all the camps.

A squirrel debates whether nuts need a hat,
While the wise old owl just chuckles at that.
Dandelions puff like fluffy clouds,
Whispering jokes to the gathering crowds.

So raise your glass to the laughter we share,
In this patch of green, without a care.
Each breath fills our hearts with carefree delight,
In a world bursting forth, full of pure light!

Aromatic Tales of Old

Once in a pot, a bean dreamed of brew,
With hopes of becoming an espresso too!
A whiff of vanilla, a dash of thrill,
Each aroma crafting stories, what a skill!

Cinnamon spins tales of winters past,
While thyme jokes that it's never outclassed.
Cloves are the poets, witty and bright,
Reciting verses in the soft moonlight.

Ginger leaps up with a twist and a turn,
Its spicy charm leaves us eager to learn.
Peppercorns giggle in a peppery haze,
Trading recipes and aromatic praise.

With each gentle whiff, we roll with glee,
On a culinary journey, come join me!
In the spice of life, let humor unfold,
These aromatic tales are pure gold!

Chilled Reflections in Glass

A glass of delight with a twist of lime,
Tells the tales of a summer time.
Ice cubes laughing, all stacked in a row,
While mint leaves dance like they're ready to go!

Sip the sunshine, bright and bold,
With stories of joy that never get old.
The straw is a bridge to the fun we seek,
Where flavors collide in a playful peek.

Giggling bubbles rise to the top,
As flavors burst forth, they won't stop!
Lemon has jokes that tickle the taste,
While green hues swirl, not a moment to waste.

Let's clink our glasses, resplendent and round,
In this chilled moment, happiness found.
With laughter and cheer, let the sips flow,
In reflections so vibrant, forever aglow!

Verdant Reminiscence

In the garden where laughter grows,
I tripped over gnomes, in sun's warm glow.
Chasing shadows, I danced through the haze,
Whispers of herbs set my heart ablaze.

The chives whispered secrets under the moon,
While sage shared tales of a kooky raccoon.
I swear that thyme winked as I rolled by,
With basil's jokes, oh my goodness, why?

The rosemary twirled, what a sight to see!
While dill did a jig, just as spry as could be.
In this leafy realm, we laughed till we cried,
Time stood still, we were all just side by side.

So here's to the plants who make life a spree,
Each leaf a chapter, life's funny decree.
With roots that entwine in our fondest gleams,
We'll savor the joy in our freshest dreams.

Tangled in the Leaves

Among tangled branches, what a delight,
I found a squirrel who was quite the sight.
He wore a tiny hat and danced on the branch,
Inviting me over for a silly prance.

With minty breath and a cheeky grin,
He told me of mischief, where to begin?
The leaves held their laughter, a rustling cheer,
As I joined the party with nibbles of beer.

The parsley was gossiping, laced with a joke,
While thyme was the bard who could never be broke.
We wove tales of daring and feathery flight,
Under a canopy, so perfectly bright.

Yet by dusk, we were tangled, oh what a mess,
Clinging to stories and sweet happiness.
With leaves in my hair and a grin with no cease,
I promised this magic would never decrease.

Stories in a Sprig

In the backyard, I found a sprig,
It raised its voice, asked me to dig.
With a wink it began to unravel,
Tales of a snail and a dandy gravel.

Each leaf whispered secrets from days gone by,
A grapevine's giggle, a tomato's sigh.
They spoke of the sun and the rain's wild dance,
How they grew up together in joyful romance.

Basil laughed loud, full of spicy delight,
While cilantro added a twist in the night.
With each tiny story, I felt like a child,
As they charmed me with antics, so silly and wild.

So here's to the green, the laughter it brews,
With every fresh sprig, a dose of good news.
These memories sprightly, as bright as a star,
Will dance in my heart, forever bizarre.

The Aroma of Yesterdays

In the air, a scent of the days gone by,
A whiff of silly times that make me sigh.
With marjoram giggles and dill's witty chat,
The fragrant nostalgia made me tip my hat.

I strolled past thyme, who recited a tale,
Of a dragonfly caught in a haphazard gale.
It swayed on sweet clover, playing hide and seek,
While violets laughed with their newfound peak.

The minty breeze teased my senses to play,
Bringing memories bright, shining humor's gay.
The past is a banquet with flavors so bold,
Stories fresh picked, ready to unfold.

So raise up a glass to the scent of pure fun,
As leaves stir the laughter beneath the sun.
With each fragrant memory, here's what I'll do,
Dance through my dreams, both frothy and new.

Fresh Chronicles

Once I found a snack so bright,
It danced with laughter in the night.
A minty leaf, with a funny grin,
Whispered secrets of where it had been.

The squirrels gathered round my chair,
In disbelief of my newfound flair.
They nibbled bits, and soon enough,
We shared some quirks, all silly stuff.

A cake made out of leafy dreams,
With frosting that glows and softly gleams.
We laughed until the sun was set,
And vowed we'd never forget yet.

So here's to greens that tickle our nose,
With fleeting tales of joy that flows.
In every crunch, a giggle caught,
In every bite, sweet laughter taught.

Glimmers of Garden Light

In the garden where the sun does peek,
A tiny frog sings, or so they speak.
With legs so long and jumps so grand,
He croaks out tales of froggy land.

The daisies giggle, the petals sway,
As bunnies hop in a cheeky play.
They whisper secrets in the breeze,
Of minty finds beneath the trees.

A squirrel dons a tiny hat,
Telling folks he's chubby and plump as that.
He juggles nuts with utmost flair,
While dandelions dance without a care.

Even bugs join in for the fun,
With tiny trumpets, they've all begun.
In glimmers bright, they sing till dark,
Leaving us with a park of sparks.

Tales Beneath the Canopy

Beneath the leaves, where shadows play,
A tale unfolds in a quirky way.
An old raccoon with a brilliant hat,
Swears up and down he once caught a cat.

The owl just chuckles with knowing eyes,
While fireflies dance like little spies.
They flash a light, and with a wink,
Bring laughter in every playful blink.

Each acorn drops with a bouncing tune,
As branches sway under the moon.
A magpie joins, with its hoot and flap,
Taking the lead in this joyous chap.

So gather round, and lend an ear,
To stories wild, absurd, yet dear.
For laughter reigns beneath the trees,
In tales told soft upon the breeze.

Untold Tendrils of the Past

In the attic, dust dances round,
Where memories linger and laughter's found.
A jar of sweets with a minty twist,
Whispers tales that we can't resist.

Grandma's recipes in a faded book,
Curly tendrils in every nook.
Her cookies giggle, her cakes would sing,
With flavors that made our hearts take wing.

There's a photo of me with a face of green,
Caught mid-bite; what a silly scene!
With frosting smeared across my cheek,
I laugh at the past; oh, wasn't it sleek?

So here's to the moments tucked away,
In every sprig, in every play.
The tendrils twist, but joy stays fast,
In memories sweet, forever cast.

Garden Secrets

In a patch of green, weeds do hide,
A rogue tomato, in pride, does bide.
I whisper to the zucchini, it's true,
'You've got more flair than me, who knew?'

The carrots gossip, with roots so deep,
While crickets hop, and the lettuce peep.
A sneaky squirrel, with a stash so bold,
Claims stripes of brown for some coveted gold.

Butterflies dance around the thyme,
While bees do plot a heist in rhyme.
I tell my secrets to the rain,
With every drop, it brings a gain.

So come take a look, just don't be shy,
In this patch, all the veggies fly.
With laughter sprouting from every seed,
The garden whispers, come take the lead!

Reflections in a Cool Shade

Under the tree, where the cool winds muse,
   I find a chair with funky views.
  The squirrels hold meetings, all in a row,
   Debating the best nut for squirrel show.

  A sundial giggles, ticking the hours,
As shadows play games amidst the flowers.
    I sip my drink, flavors collide,
  While ants march on, never to hide.

The grass whispers gossip of tomfoolery,
   As birds chirp tales of their foolery.
    The breeze tickles as if to say,
  In life's cool shade, wackiness stays.

  So linger long under branches wide,
For laughter blooms where plants abide.
  With nature's giggles casting a spell,
   This silly refuge, we know it well!

Dreams Brought to Life

Dreams sprinkled with sugar and zest,
Dance along like a jolly jest.
Imagination floats like a kite,
In a world where nonsense feels just right.

A cupcake castle with frosting towers,
Where gummy bears dance in sunlit hours.
Jellybeans burst with powerful flair,
While licorice vines twirl without a care.

As rainbows spill over marshmallow hills,
And chocolate rivers bring giggling thrills.
I sneak a taste, oh what a delight,
In this world, everything feels so light.

So dream awake, let laughter flow,
Where silly tales and wishes grow.
In this land, let your spirit twine,
For in laughter's arms, we all shall shine!

Summer's Scented Echo

In the air, a whiff of fun,
Bubblegum clouds, a race to run.
Popsicle drips, oh what a taste,
In summer's grip, let no drop waste.

A caper of ants, with their sweet parade,
While kids in the park play charades.
Lemonade stands, all quench and cheer,
With sips of joy that draw us near.

Fireflies blink like little stars,
As laughter travels through soundless cars.
The warmth of sunshine, a fluffy embrace,
Summers fade gently, at a playful pace.

So grasp this moment, let it be bold,
With smiles as bright as the sunlit gold.
In echoes of laughter, memory stays,
For summertime is a festival of plays!

Enchanted Past amidst Leaves

In a garden full of dreams, I stumbled,
Where laughter floated like sweet cream.
A breeze tickled tales from days gone by,
Chasing squirrels that danced and sighed.

I tripped on a branch, fell with a thud,
And landed in a puddle of mud.
The leaves, they giggled—a rustling cheer,
While I mumbled softly, 'Well, this is queer!'

With every bite of the herbs on the ground,
Nostalgia's aroma all around.
Each taste a joke from the past we shared,
Leaves winking slyly, our secrets bared.

So here I sit, in this leafy maze,
Recalling the folly of youthful days.
No map needed, just laughter and cheer,
In this enchanted past, I've nothing to fear.

Time in a Leafy Sip

On sunny days, I sipped and swayed,
A drink that yielded memories made.
Lemonade mixed with whispers of grass,
Every sip told tales, flying past.

Friends gathered round in a sunlit spot,
Drinks in hand, oh, the people we've sought!
With each gulp, a giggle, a chortle or two,
As flavors danced like a light-hearted crew.

A splash of mint made the laughter glow,
In that leafy cup, our spirits would flow.
We toasted to summers and days we mishandled,
While the garden critters cheered with their scandal.

As time drifts on, memories blur,
Every blended sip, a playful whirr.
The leafy concoctions, in flavors we trust,
In this joyful garden, it's always a must.

The Garden's Tender Reminders

In a patch of greens, where the daisies joke,
I found a whisper of mint in the smoke.
Each bloom was a story, each leaf a laugh,
Recalling the days of the garden's craft.

The sunflowers chuckled with their golden pride,
As I danced with a lilac, arms open wide.
Bumblebees buzzing in a humorous spree,
Pink petals falling like confetti at tea.

I wandered through rows of witty old thyme,
In the garden's embrace, I felt so sublime.
Lilies were gossiping, coy and sedate,
While I marveled at flowers who never were late.

With every reminder of joyous delight,
A giggle escaped in the warm summer night.
The garden's charm wrapped us ever so tight,
In a tangle of laughter, we twinkled with light.

Flavors that Linger

In my kitchen, concoctions await,
Flavors that dance, they tantalize fate.
Chopping and chopping, a slice of surprise,
Every taste testing, a giggle that flies.

A pinch of this, a dash of that,
Creating delights where we all sat.
Rosemary sprigs in the cookies I bake,
'They're savory snacks or a brave mistake?'

Mint leaves had tumbled from drawer to floor,
Found in the mix—oh, the laughter it bore!
A taste of the past in my culinary spree,
As friends rolled in, wanting more of the glee.

With flavors that linger on tongues and in hearts,
Each bite a chuckle, where joy never parts.
In my funny kitchen, smiles are the best,
Where flavors and laughter join hands for a fest.

When Dreams Were Cooler

In the days of youthful schemes,
Where every whim was bursting at the seams,
We chased the ice cream trucks with glee,
Surrounded by sugar, wild and free.

We made up rules for silly games,
Invented oddball nicknames and claims,
Our laughter echoed down the street,
Where joy and chaos would always meet.

The pranks we pulled were truly bold,
Like sneaky ninjas, fearless and cold,
With popsicles as our secret spies,
Under a sky of raspberry pies.

Now I smile at those frosty nights,
When our hearts danced with pure delights,
A tapestry of frosted cheer,
That fills my soul throughout the year.

A Symphony of Scented Days

Whispers of mint waft through the air,
As we rolled through summers without a care,
Sundaes melting on our hungry plates,
Time flew by like happy, clumsy skates.

The neighbor's cat, the star of the show,
Chased after our shadows, oh, how they'd flow!
With laughter ringing from dusk till dawn,
A symphony of scents, always drawn.

We'd gather daisies, bizarre and bright,
Turning the ordinary into pure delight,
Dancing with joy, a curious chase,
As minty breezes whispered in grace.

Those fragrant days, oh how they gleamed,
In the garden of life, we wildly dreamed,
With every breath, a chuckle, a sigh,
Where memories minty still flutter by.

Frosty Breaths in Evening Light

In twilight hours, we'd sit and freeze,
With frosty treats and buzzing bees,
Each breath was a puff of chilly joy,
Where we spun tales, a creative ploy.

The laughter bounced off snow-covered lanes,
Like a chorus of quirks erupted in chains,
Sweaters tangled about pajama days,
With jokes and giggles in goofy ways.

We'd take a deep breath, whisper our dreams,
And prance like penguins, bursting at the seams,
In the cool of the night, under twinkling stars,
Every frosty moment could rival guitars.

So here's to those nights, unpredictable, fun,
With frosty breaths and memories spun,
We painted our nights with laughter and cheer,
Creating a warmth we still hold dear.

Limelight Lulls of the Past

In the limelight, we danced with flair,
Dramatic stunts with minty air,
We'd reenact scenes from our favorite shows,
As ice cream melted, excitement arose.

The laughter shared was the best kind,
And those little mishaps, we didn't mind,
A face splashed with whipped cream's delight,
Turned all our blunders into pure light.

With twinkling candles and wishes made,
We'd pick our favorites, never afraid,
To jump on tables and proclaim a song,
For all the moments, we couldn't go wrong!

Now I cherish those limelight lulls,
In a world of mint that pleasantly pulls,
Guiding my heart back to youthful glee,
Where every mishap was pure jubilee.

Mint-Kissed Reveries

A sprig of green, a tale unfolds,
Of summer days when laughter holds.
With icy treats and winks so sly,
We danced beneath the open sky.

The garden's jokes were fresh and bright,
As fireflies joined us, twinkling light.
We'd steal the sun, then share a grin,
For every sip, a laugh within.

Remembering those silly dares,
To chase the breeze while twisting hairs.
With sticky hands and joyful mess,
We'd claim the world — a soft caress.

Now minty dreams make mornings sweet,
As echoes of our past retreat.
With every breath, a chuckle's trace,
In fragrant moments, we embrace.

The Touch of Summer's Hand

A gentle breeze begins to tease,
With playful whispers through the trees.
The sun, a cheeky golden lad,
Invites us out to play — so mad!

We make a splash, a fruity cheer,
With silly songs that only we hear.
The melting cones down shirt fronts glide,
As soda laughter bubbles wide.

We build our ship from couch and cloth,
Set sail for realms where socks do froth.
With every wave, a giggle's glow,
In summers long past, oh how we'd go!

Now memories swirl like fizzy sodas,
Each sip a cheer for silly odas.
In sunny climes where giggles blend,
Our tales, like breezes, never end.

Sweet Notes from the Past

In cookie crumbles, stories hide,
With sprinkles bright, we take a ride.
A world of flavors, each bite a cheer,
Past pleasures dance, so sweet and clear.

We'd sing of days when skies were blue,
With candy dreams and friends so true.
Jellybean laughter fills the air,
As we reminisce without a care.

Remember when we dared to bake,
Yet ended up with a gooey quake?
That flour fight, a powdery spree,
Resulted in giggles—just you and me.

Now tasty echoes form a tune,
That flutters softly 'neath the moon.
In every crumb, a joy replays,
Sweet notes that brighten all our days.

Essence of Whimsy

A dash of fun, a swirl of spice,
With silly hats that look so nice.
We prance around like tea-time gnomes,
In whimsical hats and our crazy homes.

The pop of fizz, a joyful shout,
With bubbles playing hide and doubt.
We'd chase our tails and catch some breeze,
With giggles growing like the trees.

Each moment crisp, like minty air,
With every flake of laughter rare.
We'd draw mustaches on the cats,
And dance with chairs, oh silly chats!

As time goes by, we laugh anew,
In wrinkled tales, our laughter grew.
In every twist, the joy persists,
In quirky ways, we can't resist!

Sweetness of Forgotten Days

We danced with shadows in the breeze,
Chasing giggles, with such ease.
A chocolate fountain flowed nearby,
Lollipop dreams that made us fly.

We wore our hats, so far off-kilter,
Twirling in dresses, no time to filter.
A slip, a fall, we cried with glee,
Splashing in puddles, wild and free.

Our secrets whispered on the floor,
Silly thoughts we just adored.
With friends who'd sing off-tune and loud,
In our silly world, we were so proud.

So here's to the days we can't replace,
To joyful times we can still chase.
Each chuckle, a treasure, tucked away,
In the sweetness of those forgotten days.

Lush Recollections

Remember the grass that tickled our toes,
Each prank and giggle, as everybody knows?
Fumbled high-fives, and awkward falls,
Chasing the ice cream truck's jolly calls.

Bubbles that popped, raising a cheer,
Conversations with bugs, so weirdly clear.
Crayons and paper, all mismatched hues,
Creating great art, with our trusty glues.

With marshmallow fights and sugary snacks,
Filling our backpacks with love and laughs.
The world was huge, and we were brave,
In gardens of joy, our memories wave.

So let's toast those days, so lush and bright,
Where chaos reigned in pure delight.
With every laugh and silly plan,
We lived out dreams, as only we can.

Breezes of Youth

In the morning sun, we'd run so wild,
With the spirit and joy of a carefree child.
Each breeze carried laughter, so light and sweet,
As we danced in circles, skipping our feet.

We tried to fly with makeshift wings,
Pretending to soar, oh such silly things!
With twigs for swords and crowns of leaves,
Claiming the backyard, our kingdom achieved.

Sharing secrets beneath the tree,
Giggles and whispers only we could see.
Our fortress built with laughter and glee,
On branches of dreams, we felt so free.

So here's to those breezes, so crisp and bright,
A time when the world was pure delight.
With every grin, our hearts would bloom,
In the joy of youth, we found our room.

Evocations of the Herb

On sunny days, we'd play with zest,
Hiding 'neath leaves, giving our best.
Whispers of sage in the afternoon air,
As we spun around without a care.

The smell of thyme in a pot by the door,
Made our imaginations soar and roar.
With rosemary crowns, we felt divine,
Playing at kingdoms, like sunshine wine.

We tasted dreams in every leaf,
Slightly bizarre, but oh, such relief!
With minty giggles and laughter we'd weave,
In fragrant gardens, we'd never leave.

So remember the herbs and their playful charms,
Their scents bewitching, with all their harms.
In the garden of joy, where we once swirled,
Evocations of the herb filled our world.

Ephemeral Laughter of the Ages

A giggle from the past, so sweet,
In my grandma's shoes, I tap my feet.
Jokes from olden times still play,
Echoes of laughter light the way.

Tickling my ribs with memories,
Of pranks and pies, and silly decrees.
A wink, a nudge, the humor we share,
Unlocking joy in the thinnest air.

How foolish we looked in our tacky clothes,
Dancing like pros, but nobody knows.
In every wrinkle, a joke remains,
Time's little jest, coursing through veins.

So let's raise a glass, make a toast,
To memories funny, we cherish most.
With laughter as our lasting refrain,
We'll dance through the years, we'll giggle again.

The Zest of Time Travel

Jump in a bubble and float through the air,
Visiting decades without a care.
Pastel parties, I see, how they shimmied,
With outfits so bright, it's almost dimmed.

A robot in 2080 sings me a song,
I taught it my moves—it dances along!
With twists and flips, it churns up a scene,
Together we laugh, quite the lively machine.

Oh, how people dressed in ridiculous styles,
Big hair and platform shoes, stretching for miles.
Every era a comic, a playful delight,
Time travel's humor, bringing pure light.

So back to the present, my bubble does pop,
With laughter and zest, I can never stop.
Let history tickle; let joy interlace,
In the fabric of time, each grin finds its place.

Wandering Through Minted Moments

A stroll through laughter on a sunny street,
Finding joy in memories, oh so sweet.
Every corner hides a tale so sly,
Of quirky adventures that never die.

With gumdrops and giggles, I trip and sway,
Dodging the frowns that come out to play.
A misstep here, a chuckle there,
In the wild ride of life, nothing to spare.

Snapshots and doodles scribbled on walls,
Each sporting a punchline, as humor calls.
Walking through moments, they gleam with glee,
A candy-coated journey, just you and me.

So here's to the wander, the laughter, the cheer,
Every minted memory drawing us near.
A canvas of smiles, oh what a scene,
In this delightful world where we've always been.

Candied Memories Underfoot

Step where the licorice meets the gum,
With every squishy sound, we hum.
Crackles of laughter rise from the ground,
In this patch of sweetness, joy can be found.

Candy wrappers whisper of secrets untold,
Of tricks and treats from days of old.
With jellies and jellybeans happily strewn,
What adventures await? I swoon!

Marshmallow clouds fluff up the sky,
With peanut butter promises, oh my!
As taffy pulls tight our playful dreams,
Life's wacky humor flows in vibrant streams.

So let's skate on dreams made of frosted delight,
With giggles and grins, we dance through the night.
In candied wonder, our memories flare,
Living each moment with laughter to spare.

Fragrant Footprints in Time

I once chewed gum with flair,
It stuck like memories rare.
A minty swirl, a breath so bold,
With every smack, a tale retold.

In school, I hid it in my desk,
A secret stash, a joyous quest.
But lunchroom scents would fill the air,
I'd chew and grin, without a care.

Those fleeting days, both sweet and wild,
Like candy dreams of a laughing child.
With every giggle, a burst of zest,
In fruity fun, they were the best.

Now I laugh at what I do,
With minty puffs of memory's brew.
So here's to days that make us grin,
With fragrant footprints, let's begin!

Herbal Hues of Nostalgia

I once brewed tea with mint so bright,
A sip of joy, a sip of light.
It brewed a riot in my throat,
Surprising each unsuspecting goat.

In gardens lush, where laughter played,
I danced in hues of green displayed.
With every sneeze, the herbs would fly,
And giggles echoed to the sky.

There's something funny in the scent,
Of herbs and laughter, heaven-sent.
Each whiff a wink from days gone by,
That linger sweet like bubblegum sky.

And now I sip on memories soft,
As herbal scents lift my heart aloft.
Here's to the chuckles and giggles shared,
With every cup, our joys declared!

Crisp Leaves of Memory

In autumn's dance, the leaves would crunch,
I'd munch on snacks and laugh a bunch.
With minty breath and cheeks aglow,
I chuckled loud in nature's show.

A friend and I, in leafy capers,
With mint on our breath, we were the drapers!
We'd toss the leaves, in joy and cheer,
And inhale laughter, crystal clear.

Those days were crisp, like morning air,
With memories that spark and flare.
A gust of fun, a hint of surprise,
In each fall breeze, we'd improvise.

So here we stand, with leaves in hand,
Recalling moments that life had planned.
With every crunch, we're young once more,
Crisp leaves of laughter, we'll forever adore!

The Sweetness of Unforgotten Days

I found a jar of candy bright,
Each piece a treasure, pure delight.
With every taste, a giggle grew,
A wondrous trip, a joyful view.

Remember those times we'd sneak a chew?
With sugar highs that only flew!
In secret caves of sugary bliss,
We'd plan adventures, sealed with a kiss.

Those days were sweet, with laughter bright,
Spinning tales under stars at night.
With every giggle and candid grin,
We painted memories deep within.

Now as I savor past's embrace,
A smile appears on my face.
For in each bite, I find my way,
To sweetness found in unforgotten days!

Sprigs of Cherished Remembrance

In a garden filled with zest,
I plucked a sprig from a jest.
It whispered tales of summer nights,
And tangled in my tasty bites.

From my pockets, scents unspooled,
In salads tossed, I was quite fooled.
Laughter danced on tangy air,
Each nibble brought a cheerful stare.

When friends would come, we'd feast and share,
A little spritz, a bit of flair.
Giggles mixed with spicy crunch,
We'd sip on drinks, and munch, and munch.

Now when I pass that vibrant patch,
I chuckle at the day's big catch.
For in those leaves, a story stays,
Of silly times and fragrant ways.

Crisp Shadows on a Sundrenched Path

On a sunny stroll, I took a chance,
With a sprig of green in my pants.
Each step I took, it bounced with glee,
As if it sang along with me.

I slipped on gravel, made a blunder,
That sprig then beckoned like a thunder.
It tickled as it danced in tow,
Creating chaos, stealing the show.

A passing cat gave me a glance,
I swore it laughed at my new dance.
The sprig just giggled, holding tight,
A chirpy shadow in the light.

Now every step, it's memory bright,
Of funny slips and pure delight.
When shadows lengthen and suns retreat,
I'll laugh at life, oh, how sweet!

Fresh Echoes

In the garden where we played,
Bright green leaves made us delayed.
Echoes of laughter filled the air,
With tangy scents of joyful flair.

We munched on herbs, not a care,
Each bite released a story rare.
In every crunch, a giggle found,
As flavors twirled and danced around.

Chasing memories on a whim,
I tasted joy, I felt the brim.
A touch of mint, a zest of teens,
Made every moment burst at seams.

Now in the kitchen, pots will clank,
As I recall that leafy prank.
Fresh echoes linger, still they sing,
Of fragrant joy that summers bring.

Whispers of Green Dreams

In a world where flavors play,
I found a sprig that led the way.
It whispered secrets, bold and sweet,
With every nibble, pure delight to greet.

Green dreams danced through afternoon,
As I brewed chaos like a tune.
In every sip, a chuckle found,
Sprouting laughter from the ground.

From first fresh leaves to zesty glass,
The sprig became the star, alas!
We toasted to adventures old,
With leafy laughter, tales retold.

Those whispers linger, sweet and bright,
Creating joy in every bite.
Through greens and giggles, dreams converge,
In tasty worlds where laughs emerge.

www.ingramcontent.com/pod-product-compliance
Lightning Source LLC
Chambersburg PA
CBHW071843160426
43209CB00003B/392